Challenge Accepted!

A JOURNAL TO HELP WOMEN CONSISTENTLY ACCOMPLISH SMALL DAILY GOALS

Copyright © 2020 by Shayla McGhee
Written by Shayla McGhee

All rights reserved. No part of this book may be used or reproduced in any manner whatsoever without the prior written permission of the author.

Introduction

I created this journal to help you accomplish, overcome, and actualize small, daily goals so that you can become more productive, happy, and successful on a consistent basis.

There is something truly gratifying about setting a quick daily challenge and achieving it. That's what this journal is for!

Okay, let's talk about how to do this!

First, set a specific, personal objective that you would like to complete by the end of the day. This can be anything from exercising for 30 minutes or being kind to a grouchy coworker, to refraining from eating that bag of chips in the pantry. Whatever you choose is perfectly fine.

Just remember that you are trying to fulfill one challenge per day, so don't make it too lengthy. You've got other things to do today!

Next, briefly write down how you are going to achieve your goal in 1-5 steps. This is your plan of action. All conquerors need one. You don't have to fill out all five steps. Some challenges may only take one. Whatever it takes to finish your task, write it down.

Lastly, tell yourself why you chose this challenge. I added this section because it's always important to know why you are doing something and how it will make you a better individual. In fact, a driving purpose can motivate you even more!

Well, that's it. I sincerely hope you enjoy crushing your daily challenges!

-Shayla McGhee

DATE ___/___/___

Today I Challenge Myself To

_____
_____
_____
_____

**THE STEPS I WILL TAKE TO
CRUSH THIS CHALLENGE ARE**

1.
2.
3.
4.
5.

I CHOSE TODAY'S CHALLENGE BECAUSE

_____
_____
_____
_____

DATE ___/___/___

Today I Challenge Myself To

_____
_____
_____
_____

**THE STEPS I WILL TAKE TO
CRUSH THIS CHALLENGE ARE**

1.

2.

3.

4.

5.

I CHOSE TODAY'S CHALLENGE BECAUSE

_____
_____
_____
_____

DATE ___/___/___

Today I Challenge Myself To

_____
_____
_____
_____

THE STEPS I WILL TAKE TO CRUSH THIS CHALLENGE ARE

1.
2.
3.
4.
5.

I CHOSE TODAY'S CHALLENGE BECAUSE

_____
_____
_____
_____

DATE ___/___/___

Today I Challenge Myself To

_____
_____
_____
_____

**THE STEPS I WILL TAKE TO
CRUSH THIS CHALLENGE ARE**

1.

2.

3.

4.

5.

I CHOSE TODAY'S CHALLENGE BECAUSE

_____
_____
_____
_____
_____

DATE ___/___/___

Today I Challenge Myself To

_____
_____
_____
_____

**THE STEPS I WILL TAKE TO
CRUSH THIS CHALLENGE ARE**

1.
2.
3.
4.
5.

I CHOSE TODAY'S CHALLENGE BECAUSE

_____
_____
_____
_____

DATE ___/___/___

Today I Challenge Myself To

_____
_____
_____
_____

THE STEPS I WILL TAKE TO CRUSH THIS CHALLENGE ARE

1.

2.

3.

4.

5.

I CHOSE TODAY'S CHALLENGE BECAUSE

_____
_____
_____
_____

DATE ___/___/___

Today I Challenge Myself To

_____
_____
_____
_____
_____

THE STEPS I WILL TAKE TO CRUSH THIS CHALLENGE ARE

1.
2.
3.
4.
5.

I CHOSE TODAY'S CHALLENGE BECAUSE

_____
_____
_____
_____

DATE ___/___/___

Today I Challenge Myself To

_____
_____
_____
_____
_____

**THE STEPS I WILL TAKE TO
CRUSH THIS CHALLENGE ARE**

1.

2.

3.

4.

5.

I CHOSE TODAY'S CHALLENGE BECAUSE

_____
_____
_____
_____
_____

DATE ___/___/___

Today I Challenge Myself To

_____
_____
_____
_____

**THE STEPS I WILL TAKE TO
CRUSH THIS CHALLENGE ARE**

1.
2.
3.
4.
5.

I CHOSE TODAY'S CHALLENGE BECAUSE

_____
_____
_____
_____

DATE ___/___/___

Today I Challenge Myself To

_____
_____
_____
_____

**THE STEPS I WILL TAKE TO
CRUSH THIS CHALLENGE ARE**

1.

2.

3.

4.

5.

I CHOSE TODAY'S CHALLENGE BECAUSE

_____
_____
_____
_____

DATE ___/___/___

Today I Challenge Myself To

_____
_____
_____
_____

**THE STEPS I WILL TAKE TO
CRUSH THIS CHALLENGE ARE**

1.
2.
3.
4.
5.

I CHOSE TODAY'S CHALLENGE BECAUSE

_____
_____
_____
_____

DATE ___/___/___

Today I Challenge Myself To

_____
_____
_____
_____

**THE STEPS I WILL TAKE TO
CRUSH THIS CHALLENGE ARE**

1.

2.

3.

4.

5.

I CHOSE TODAY'S CHALLENGE BECAUSE

_____
_____
_____
_____

DATE ___/___/___

Today I Challenge Myself To

_____
_____
_____
_____
_____

**THE STEPS I WILL TAKE TO
CRUSH THIS CHALLENGE ARE**

1.

2.

3.

4.

5.

I CHOSE TODAY'S CHALLENGE BECAUSE

_____
_____
_____
_____
_____

DATE ____/____/____

Today I Challenge Myself To

_____
_____
_____
_____

**THE STEPS I WILL TAKE TO
CRUSH THIS CHALLENGE ARE**

1.

2.

3.

4.

5.

I CHOSE TODAY'S CHALLENGE BECAUSE

_____
_____
_____
_____

DATE ___/___/___

Today I Challenge Myself To

_____
_____
_____
_____

**THE STEPS I WILL TAKE TO
CRUSH THIS CHALLENGE ARE**

1.
2.
3.
4.
5.

I CHOSE TODAY'S CHALLENGE BECAUSE

_____
_____
_____
_____

DATE ___/___/___

Today I Challenge Myself To

_____
_____
_____
_____

**THE STEPS I WILL TAKE TO
CRUSH THIS CHALLENGE ARE**

1.

2.

3.

4.

5.

I CHOSE TODAY'S CHALLENGE BECAUSE

_____
_____
_____
_____

DATE ___/___/___

Today I Challenge Myself To

_____
_____
_____
_____

**THE STEPS I WILL TAKE TO
CRUSH THIS CHALLENGE ARE**

1.

2.

3.

4.

5.

I CHOSE TODAY'S CHALLENGE BECAUSE

_____
_____
_____
_____

DATE ___/___/___

Today I Challenge Myself To

_____
_____
_____
_____

**THE STEPS I WILL TAKE TO
CRUSH THIS CHALLENGE ARE**

1.

2.

3.

4.

5.

I CHOSE TODAY'S CHALLENGE BECAUSE

_____
_____
_____
_____

DATE ___/___/___

Today I Challenge Myself To

_____
_____
_____
_____
_____

**THE STEPS I WILL TAKE TO
CRUSH THIS CHALLENGE ARE**

1.

2.

3.

4.

5.

I CHOSE TODAY'S CHALLENGE BECAUSE

_____
_____
_____
_____
_____

DATE ___/___/___

Today I Challenge Myself To

_____
_____
_____
_____

**THE STEPS I WILL TAKE TO
CRUSH THIS CHALLENGE ARE**

1.

2.

3.

4.

5.

I CHOSE TODAY'S CHALLENGE BECAUSE

_____
_____
_____
_____

DATE ___/___/___

Today I Challenge Myself To

_____
_____
_____
_____

**THE STEPS I WILL TAKE TO
CRUSH THIS CHALLENGE ARE**

1.

2.

3.

4.

5.

I CHOSE TODAY'S CHALLENGE BECAUSE

_____
_____
_____
_____

DATE ___/___/___

Today I Challenge Myself To

_____
_____
_____
_____

**THE STEPS I WILL TAKE TO
CRUSH THIS CHALLENGE ARE**

1.

2.

3.

4.

5.

I CHOSE TODAY'S CHALLENGE BECAUSE

_____
_____
_____
_____
_____

DATE ___/___/___

Today I Challenge Myself To

_____
_____
_____
_____

**THE STEPS I WILL TAKE TO
CRUSH THIS CHALLENGE ARE**

1.
2.
3.
4.
5.

I CHOSE TODAY'S CHALLENGE BECAUSE

_____
_____
_____
_____

DATE ___/___/___

Today I Challenge Myself To

_____
_____
_____
_____

**THE STEPS I WILL TAKE TO
CRUSH THIS CHALLENGE ARE**

1.

2.

3.

4.

5.

I CHOSE TODAY'S CHALLENGE BECAUSE

_____
_____
_____
_____

DATE ___/___/___

Today I Challenge Myself To

_____
_____
_____
_____

THE STEPS I WILL TAKE TO CRUSH THIS CHALLENGE ARE

1.

2.

3.

4.

5.

I CHOSE TODAY'S CHALLENGE BECAUSE

_____
_____
_____
_____

DATE ___/___/___

Today I Challenge Myself To

_____
_____
_____
_____
_____

**THE STEPS I WILL TAKE TO
CRUSH THIS CHALLENGE ARE**

1.

2.

3.

4.

5.

I CHOSE TODAY'S CHALLENGE BECAUSE

_____
_____
_____
_____
_____

DATE ___/___/___

Today I Challenge Myself To

_____
_____
_____
_____

THE STEPS I WILL TAKE TO CRUSH THIS CHALLENGE ARE

1.

2.

3.

4.

5.

I CHOSE TODAY'S CHALLENGE BECAUSE

_____
_____
_____
_____

DATE ___/___/___

Today I Challenge Myself To

_____
_____
_____
_____

**THE STEPS I WILL TAKE TO
CRUSH THIS CHALLENGE ARE**

1.

2.

3.

4.

5.

I CHOSE TODAY'S CHALLENGE BECAUSE

_____
_____
_____
_____

DATE ___/___/___

Today I Challenge Myself To

_____
_____
_____
_____

**THE STEPS I WILL TAKE TO
CRUSH THIS CHALLENGE ARE**

1.
2.
3.
4.
5.

I CHOSE TODAY'S CHALLENGE BECAUSE

_____
_____
_____
_____

DATE ___/___/___

Today I Challenge Myself To

_____
_____
_____
_____
_____

**THE STEPS I WILL TAKE TO
CRUSH THIS CHALLENGE ARE**

1.

2.

3.

4.

5.

I CHOSE TODAY'S CHALLENGE BECAUSE

_____
_____
_____
_____
_____

DATE ___/___/___

Today I Challenge Myself To

_____
_____
_____
_____
_____

THE STEPS I WILL TAKE TO CRUSH THIS CHALLENGE ARE

1.
2.
3.
4.
5.

I CHOSE TODAY'S CHALLENGE BECAUSE

_____
_____
_____
_____
_____

DATE ___/___/___

Today I Challenge Myself To

_____
_____
_____
_____

**THE STEPS I WILL TAKE TO
CRUSH THIS CHALLENGE ARE**

1.

2.

3.

4.

5.

I CHOSE TODAY'S CHALLENGE BECAUSE

_____
_____
_____
_____

DATE ___/___/___

Today I Challenge Myself To

_____
_____
_____
_____

**THE STEPS I WILL TAKE TO
CRUSH THIS CHALLENGE ARE**

1.

2.

3.

4.

5.

I CHOSE TODAY'S CHALLENGE BECAUSE

_____
_____
_____
_____
_____

DATE ___/___/___

Today I Challenge Myself To

_____
_____
_____
_____

THE STEPS I WILL TAKE TO CRUSH THIS CHALLENGE ARE

1.

2.

3.

4.

5.

I CHOSE TODAY'S CHALLENGE BECAUSE

_____
_____
_____
_____

DATE ___/___/___

Today I Challenge Myself To

_____
_____
_____
_____

**THE STEPS I WILL TAKE TO
CRUSH THIS CHALLENGE ARE**

1.
2.
3.
4.
5.

I CHOSE TODAY'S CHALLENGE BECAUSE

_____
_____
_____
_____

DATE ___/___/___

Today I Challenge Myself To

_____
_____
_____
_____
_____

**THE STEPS I WILL TAKE TO
CRUSH THIS CHALLENGE ARE**

1.

2.

3.

4.

5.

I CHOSE TODAY'S CHALLENGE BECAUSE

_____
_____
_____
_____
_____

DATE ___/___/___

Today I Challenge Myself To

_____
_____
_____
_____

THE STEPS I WILL TAKE TO CRUSH THIS CHALLENGE ARE

1.
2.
3.
4.
5.

I CHOSE TODAY'S CHALLENGE BECAUSE

_____
_____
_____
_____

DATE ___/___/___

Today I Challenge Myself To

_____
_____
_____
_____

**THE STEPS I WILL TAKE TO
CRUSH THIS CHALLENGE ARE**

1.
2.
3.
4.
5.

I CHOSE TODAY'S CHALLENGE BECAUSE

_____
_____
_____
_____

DATE ____/____/____

Today I Challenge Myself To

_____
_____
_____
_____

**THE STEPS I WILL TAKE TO
CRUSH THIS CHALLENGE ARE**

1.
2.
3.
4.
5.

I CHOSE TODAY'S CHALLENGE BECAUSE

_____
_____
_____
_____

DATE ___/___/___

Today I Challenge Myself To

_____
_____
_____
_____

**THE STEPS I WILL TAKE TO
CRUSH THIS CHALLENGE ARE**

1.

2.

3.

4.

5.

I CHOSE TODAY'S CHALLENGE BECAUSE

_____
_____
_____
_____

DATE ___/___/___

Today I Challenge Myself To

_____
_____
_____
_____

**THE STEPS I WILL TAKE TO
CRUSH THIS CHALLENGE ARE**

1.

2.

3.

4.

5.

I CHOSE TODAY'S CHALLENGE BECAUSE

_____
_____
_____
_____

DATE ___/___/___

Today I Challenge Myself To

_____
_____
_____
_____

**THE STEPS I WILL TAKE TO
CRUSH THIS CHALLENGE ARE**

1.

2.

3.

4.

5.

I CHOSE TODAY'S CHALLENGE BECAUSE

_____
_____
_____
_____
_____

DATE ___/___/___

Today I Challenge Myself To

_____
_____
_____
_____

**THE STEPS I WILL TAKE TO
CRUSH THIS CHALLENGE ARE**

1.

2.

3.

4.

5.

I CHOSE TODAY'S CHALLENGE BECAUSE

_____
_____
_____
_____

DATE ___/___/___

Today I Challenge Myself To

_____
_____
_____
_____

**THE STEPS I WILL TAKE TO
CRUSH THIS CHALLENGE ARE**

1.

2.

3.

4.

5.

I CHOSE TODAY'S CHALLENGE BECAUSE

_____
_____
_____
_____
_____

DATE ___/___/___

Today I Challenge Myself To

_____
_____
_____
_____

**THE STEPS I WILL TAKE TO
CRUSH THIS CHALLENGE ARE**

1.
2.
3.
4.
5.

I CHOSE TODAY'S CHALLENGE BECAUSE

_____
_____
_____
_____

DATE ___/___/___

Today I Challenge Myself To

_____
_____
_____
_____

**THE STEPS I WILL TAKE TO
CRUSH THIS CHALLENGE ARE**

1.

2.

3.

4.

5.

I CHOSE TODAY'S CHALLENGE BECAUSE

_____
_____
_____
_____
_____

DATE ___/___/___

Today I Challenge Myself To

_____
_____
_____
_____

**THE STEPS I WILL TAKE TO
CRUSH THIS CHALLENGE ARE**

1.

2.

3.

4.

5.

I CHOSE TODAY'S CHALLENGE BECAUSE

_____
_____
_____
_____

DATE ___/___/___

Today I Challenge Myself To

_____
_____
_____
_____

**THE STEPS I WILL TAKE TO
CRUSH THIS CHALLENGE ARE**

1.

2.

3.

4.

5.

I CHOSE TODAY'S CHALLENGE BECAUSE

_____
_____
_____
_____

DATE ___/___/___

Today I Challenge Myself To

_____
_____
_____
_____

THE STEPS I WILL TAKE TO CRUSH THIS CHALLENGE ARE

1.
2.
3.
4.
5.

I CHOSE TODAY'S CHALLENGE BECAUSE

_____
_____
_____
_____

DATE ___/___/___

Today I Challenge Myself To

_____
_____
_____
_____

**THE STEPS I WILL TAKE TO
CRUSH THIS CHALLENGE ARE**

1.

2.

3.

4.

5.

I CHOSE TODAY'S CHALLENGE BECAUSE

_____
_____
_____
_____

DATE ___/___/___

Today I Challenge Myself To

_____
_____
_____
_____

**THE STEPS I WILL TAKE TO
CRUSH THIS CHALLENGE ARE**

1.
2.
3.
4.
5.

I CHOSE TODAY'S CHALLENGE BECAUSE

_____
_____
_____
_____

DATE ___/___/___

Today I Challenge Myself To

_____
_____
_____
_____
_____

**THE STEPS I WILL TAKE TO
CRUSH THIS CHALLENGE ARE**

1.

2.

3.

4.

5.

I CHOSE TODAY'S CHALLENGE BECAUSE

_____
_____
_____
_____

DATE ___/___/___

Today I Challenge Myself To

_____
_____
_____
_____

THE STEPS I WILL TAKE TO CRUSH THIS CHALLENGE ARE

1.
2.
3.
4.
5.

I CHOSE TODAY'S CHALLENGE BECAUSE

_____
_____
_____
_____

DATE ____/____/____

Today I Challenge Myself To

**THE STEPS I WILL TAKE TO
CRUSH THIS CHALLENGE ARE**

1.

2.

3.

4.

5.

I CHOSE TODAY'S CHALLENGE BECAUSE

DATE ___/___/___

Today I Challenge Myself To

_____
_____
_____
_____
_____

**THE STEPS I WILL TAKE TO
CRUSH THIS CHALLENGE ARE**

1.

2.

3.

4.

5.

I CHOSE TODAY'S CHALLENGE BECAUSE

_____
_____
_____
_____
_____

DATE ____/____/____

Today I Challenge Myself To

_____
_____
_____
_____

**THE STEPS I WILL TAKE TO
CRUSH THIS CHALLENGE ARE**

1.

2.

3.

4.

5.

I CHOSE TODAY'S CHALLENGE BECAUSE

_____
_____
_____
_____

DATE ___/___/___

Today I Challenge Myself To

_____
_____
_____
_____

**THE STEPS I WILL TAKE TO
CRUSH THIS CHALLENGE ARE**

1.
2.
3.
4.
5.

I CHOSE TODAY'S CHALLENGE BECAUSE

_____
_____
_____
_____

DATE ___/___/___

Today I Challenge Myself To

_____
_____
_____
_____

**THE STEPS I WILL TAKE TO
CRUSH THIS CHALLENGE ARE**

1.

2.

3.

4.

5.

I CHOSE TODAY'S CHALLENGE BECAUSE

_____
_____
_____
_____
_____

DATE ___/___/___

Today I Challenge Myself To

_____
_____
_____
_____

THE STEPS I WILL TAKE TO CRUSH THIS CHALLENGE ARE

1.
2.
3.
4.
5.

I CHOSE TODAY'S CHALLENGE BECAUSE

_____
_____
_____
_____

DATE ___/___/___

Today I Challenge Myself To

_____
_____
_____
_____

**THE STEPS I WILL TAKE TO
CRUSH THIS CHALLENGE ARE**

1.

2.

3.

4.

5.

I CHOSE TODAY'S CHALLENGE BECAUSE

_____
_____
_____
_____
_____

DATE ___/___/___

Today I Challenge Myself To

_____
_____
_____
_____

THE STEPS I WILL TAKE TO CRUSH THIS CHALLENGE ARE

1.

2.

3.

4.

5.

I CHOSE TODAY'S CHALLENGE BECAUSE

_____
_____
_____
_____

DATE ___ / ___ / ___

Today I Challenge Myself To

_____
_____
_____
_____

**THE STEPS I WILL TAKE TO
CRUSH THIS CHALLENGE ARE**

1.

2.

3.

4.

5.

I CHOSE TODAY'S CHALLENGE BECAUSE

_____
_____
_____
_____
_____

DATE ___/___/___

Today I Challenge Myself To

_____
_____
_____
_____

THE STEPS I WILL TAKE TO CRUSH THIS CHALLENGE ARE

1.
2.
3.
4.
5.

I CHOSE TODAY'S CHALLENGE BECAUSE

_____
_____
_____
_____

DATE ___/___/___

Today I Challenge Myself To

**THE STEPS I WILL TAKE TO
CRUSH THIS CHALLENGE ARE**

1.
2.
3.
4.
5.

I CHOSE TODAY'S CHALLENGE BECAUSE

DATE ___/___/___

Today I Challenge Myself To

_____
_____
_____
_____

**THE STEPS I WILL TAKE TO
CRUSH THIS CHALLENGE ARE**

1.

2.

3.

4.

5.

I CHOSE TODAY'S CHALLENGE BECAUSE

_____
_____
_____
_____

DATE ___/___/___

Today I Challenge Myself To

_____
_____
_____
_____

**THE STEPS I WILL TAKE TO
CRUSH THIS CHALLENGE ARE**

1.

2.

3.

4.

5.

I CHOSE TODAY'S CHALLENGE BECAUSE

_____
_____
_____
_____

DATE ___/___/___

Today I Challenge Myself To

_____
_____
_____
_____

THE STEPS I WILL TAKE TO CRUSH THIS CHALLENGE ARE

1.
2.
3.
4.
5.

I CHOSE TODAY'S CHALLENGE BECAUSE

_____
_____
_____
_____

DATE ___/___/___

Today I Challenge Myself To

_____
_____
_____
_____

**THE STEPS I WILL TAKE TO
CRUSH THIS CHALLENGE ARE**

1.

2.

3.

4.

5.

I CHOSE TODAY'S CHALLENGE BECAUSE

_____
_____
_____
_____
_____

DATE ___/___/___

Today I Challenge Myself To

_____
_____
_____
_____

THE STEPS I WILL TAKE TO CRUSH THIS CHALLENGE ARE

1.
2.
3.
4.
5.

I CHOSE TODAY'S CHALLENGE BECAUSE

_____
_____
_____
_____

DATE ___/___/___

Today I Challenge Myself To

_____
_____
_____
_____

**THE STEPS I WILL TAKE TO
CRUSH THIS CHALLENGE ARE**

1.

2.

3.

4.

5.

I CHOSE TODAY'S CHALLENGE BECAUSE

_____
_____
_____
_____
_____

DATE ___/___/___

Today I Challenge Myself To

_____
_____
_____
_____

THE STEPS I WILL TAKE TO CRUSH THIS CHALLENGE ARE

1.
2.
3.
4.
5.

I CHOSE TODAY'S CHALLENGE BECAUSE

_____
_____
_____
_____

DATE ___/___/___

Today I Challenge Myself To

_____
_____
_____
_____
_____

**THE STEPS I WILL TAKE TO
CRUSH THIS CHALLENGE ARE**

1.

2.

3.

4.

5.

I CHOSE TODAY'S CHALLENGE BECAUSE

_____
_____
_____
_____
_____

DATE ___/___/___

Today I Challenge Myself To

_____
_____
_____
_____

**THE STEPS I WILL TAKE TO
CRUSH THIS CHALLENGE ARE**

1.

2.

3.

4.

5.

I CHOSE TODAY'S CHALLENGE BECAUSE

_____
_____
_____
_____

DATE ___/___/___

Today I Challenge Myself To

_____
_____
_____
_____

**THE STEPS I WILL TAKE TO
CRUSH THIS CHALLENGE ARE**

1.

2.

3.

4.

5.

I CHOSE TODAY'S CHALLENGE BECAUSE

_____
_____
_____
_____
_____

DATE ___/___/___

Today I Challenge Myself To

_____
_____
_____
_____

THE STEPS I WILL TAKE TO CRUSH THIS CHALLENGE ARE

1.

2.

3.

4.

5.

I CHOSE TODAY'S CHALLENGE BECAUSE

_____
_____
_____
_____

DATE ___/___/___

Today I Challenge Myself To

_____
_____
_____
_____

**THE STEPS I WILL TAKE TO
CRUSH THIS CHALLENGE ARE**

1.

2.

3.

4.

5.

I CHOSE TODAY'S CHALLENGE BECAUSE

_____
_____
_____
_____
_____

DATE ___/___/___

Today I Challenge Myself To

_____
_____
_____
_____

THE STEPS I WILL TAKE TO CRUSH THIS CHALLENGE ARE

1.
2.
3.
4.
5.

I CHOSE TODAY'S CHALLENGE BECAUSE

_____
_____
_____
_____

DATE ___/___/___

Today I Challenge Myself To

_____
_____
_____
_____

THE STEPS I WILL TAKE TO CRUSH THIS CHALLENGE ARE

1.

2.

3.

4.

5.

I CHOSE TODAY'S CHALLENGE BECAUSE

_____
_____
_____
_____

DATE ___/___/___

Today I Challenge Myself To

_____
_____
_____
_____

THE STEPS I WILL TAKE TO CRUSH THIS CHALLENGE ARE

1.

2.

3.

4.

5.

I CHOSE TODAY'S CHALLENGE BECAUSE

_____
_____
_____
_____
_____

DATE ___/___/___

Today I Challenge Myself To

_____
_____
_____
_____

**THE STEPS I WILL TAKE TO
CRUSH THIS CHALLENGE ARE**

1.

2.

3.

4.

5.

I CHOSE TODAY'S CHALLENGE BECAUSE

_____
_____
_____
_____

DATE ___/___/___

Today I Challenge Myself To

_____
_____
_____
_____

THE STEPS I WILL TAKE TO CRUSH THIS CHALLENGE ARE

1.
2.
3.
4.
5.

I CHOSE TODAY'S CHALLENGE BECAUSE

_____
_____
_____
_____

DATE ___/___/___

Today I Challenge Myself To

_____
_____
_____
_____

**THE STEPS I WILL TAKE TO
CRUSH THIS CHALLENGE ARE**

1.

2.

3.

4.

5.

I CHOSE TODAY'S CHALLENGE BECAUSE

_____
_____
_____
_____

DATE ___/___/___

Today I Challenge Myself To

_____
_____
_____
_____
_____

**THE STEPS I WILL TAKE TO
CRUSH THIS CHALLENGE ARE**

1.
2.
3.
4.
5.

I CHOSE TODAY'S CHALLENGE BECAUSE

_____
_____
_____
_____

DATE ___/___/___

Today I Challenge Myself To

_____
_____
_____
_____

**THE STEPS I WILL TAKE TO
CRUSH THIS CHALLENGE ARE**

1.

2.

3.

4.

5.

I CHOSE TODAY'S CHALLENGE BECAUSE

_____
_____
_____
_____

DATE ___/___/___

Today I Challenge Myself To

_____
_____
_____
_____

**THE STEPS I WILL TAKE TO
CRUSH THIS CHALLENGE ARE**

1.

2.

3.

4.

5.

I CHOSE TODAY'S CHALLENGE BECAUSE

_____
_____
_____
_____

DATE ___/___/___

Today I Challenge Myself To

_____
_____
_____
_____

**THE STEPS I WILL TAKE TO
CRUSH THIS CHALLENGE ARE**

1.

2.

3.

4.

5.

I CHOSE TODAY'S CHALLENGE BECAUSE

_____
_____
_____
_____
_____

DATE ___/___/___

Today I Challenge Myself To

_____
_____
_____
_____

**THE STEPS I WILL TAKE TO
CRUSH THIS CHALLENGE ARE**

1.
2.
3.
4.
5.

I CHOSE TODAY'S CHALLENGE BECAUSE

_____
_____
_____
_____

DATE ___/___/___

Today I Challenge Myself To

_____
_____
_____
_____

**THE STEPS I WILL TAKE TO
CRUSH THIS CHALLENGE ARE**

1.
2.
3.
4.
5.

I CHOSE TODAY'S CHALLENGE BECAUSE

_____
_____
_____
_____
_____

DATE ___/___/___

Today I Challenge Myself To

_____
_____
_____
_____

**THE STEPS I WILL TAKE TO
CRUSH THIS CHALLENGE ARE**

1.
2.
3.
4.
5.

I CHOSE TODAY'S CHALLENGE BECAUSE

_____
_____
_____
_____

DATE ___/___/___

Today I Challenge Myself To

_____
_____
_____
_____

THE STEPS I WILL TAKE TO CRUSH THIS CHALLENGE ARE

1.

2.

3.

4.

5.

I CHOSE TODAY'S CHALLENGE BECAUSE

_____
_____
_____
_____

Made in the USA
Columbia, SC
10 February 2022